RUBANK EDUCATIONAL
LIBRARY No. 145

ONLINE MEDIA INCLUDED
Audio Recordings
Printable Piano Accompaniments

Concert and Contest COLLECTION

for **C FLUTE**

with piano accompaniment
Compiled and Edited
by **H. VOXMAN**

PLAYBACK+
Speed · Pitch · Balance · Loop

To access recordings and PDF accompaniments visit:
www.halleonard.com/mylibrary

2735-4631-2218-5323

ISBN 978-1-4234-7717-4

RUBANK®

HAL•LEONARD®
7777 W. BLUEMOUND RD. P.O. BOX 13819 MILWAUKEE, WI 53213

Visit Hal Leonard Online at
www.halleonard.com

Contents

CONCERT AND CONTEST COLLECTION for Flute

Gavotte

Flute

FR. JOS. GOSSEC
Edited by H. Voxman

Copyright MCMXLIX by Rubank, Inc., Chicago, Ill.
International Copyright Secured

Bergamask

Flute

PAUL KOEPKE
Edited by H. Voxman

5

Serenade

Flute

VICTOR HERBERT, Op. 3
Edited by H. Voxman

Scherzino

Flute

JOACHIM ANDERSEN, Op. 55, No. 6
Edited by H. Voxman

Flute

Valse Gracieuse

Flute

W. POPP, Op. 261, No. 2
Edited by H. Voxman

Flute

Andalouse

Flute

ÉMILE PESSARD, Op. 20
Edited by H. Voxman

11
Flute

Menuet

from

L'Arlésienne Suite No. 2

Flute

GEORGES BIZET
Edited by H. Voxman

13
Flute

Serenade

Flute

JOS. HAYDN
Edited by H. Voxman

Andante cantabile

Siciliana and Giga
from
Sonata V

Flute

G. F. HANDEL
Edited by H. Voxman

Menuet and Spirit Dance

from Orpheus

C. W. von GLUCK
Edited by H. Voxman

Flute

Polonaise and Badinerie
from
Suite in B Minor

Flute

J. S. BACH
Edited by H. Voxman

Flute

Romance

Flute

GEORGES BRUN, Op. 41
Edited by H. Voxman

Flight of the Bumblebee

from
The Legend of the Czar Sultan

Flute

N. RIMSKY-KORSAKOFF
Edited by H. Voxman

Flute

PAN!

Flute

Pastorale

J. DONJON
Edited by H. Voxman